WORK

Brief glimpses
of the Poor Law
and
life inside
Clutton Union-house

by
Ken Griffiths

FIDUCIA PRESS
2005

WORKHOUSE

Brief glimpses of the Poor Law
and life inside
Clutton Union-house

by
Ken Griffiths

Book Design
Roy Gallop Ken Griffiths
Typing Services Leighanne Gough
Photographs Carol Griffiths

Front cover: *This engraving by Thomas Bewick (1753-1828) reflects the hardships endured by the rural poor as a result of enclosures, which forced many into the new workhouses.*

Title page: *Begging was seen by many as an alternative to the harsh regime of the workhouse imposed by the New Poor Law, particularly in its early days.*

Back cover: *Rural evictions were often the consequence of enclosures, the biggest single theft from the people in our history.*

Published by Fiducia Press, 10 Fairfield Road, Southville, Bristol, BS3 1NG.
Copyright © Ken Griffiths.

Fiducia Press ISBN O 946217 20 3
Printed in Great Britain by Doveton Press Ltd., Bristol

The aim of this booklet is to present 'snapshots' of the Poor Law and Clutton workhouse. This account should be looked upon only as an introduction to the subject. For those who wish to know more of the history, structure and the day to day running of the workhouse I respectfully refer them to *The Poor Law and the Clutton Union* by Dr. Charles Chillcott and *The Cambrook House Story* by David Jones.

Both publications are available for study in the Somerset Studies section of Taunton Public Library.

Works I have consulted during the preparation of this study have included:

The Clutton Union Archive, courtesy of Somerset Record Office.

The Poor Law and the Clutton Union by Dr Charles Chillcott, 1996.

The Cambrook House Story by David Jones, 1996.

Articles from *The Countryman* and *Country Origins*.

A Social and Economic History of Britain by S.L. Case and D.J.Hall. Edward Arnold (Publishers)Ltd., London, 1977 (1983 edition used).

The History Today Companion to British History, edited by Juliet Gardiner and Neil Wenborn. Collins and Brown Ltd., London,1995.

The Age of Reform by Llewellyn Woodward. Oxford University Press, 1938 (1992 edition used).

A Country Camera 1844-1914 by Gordon Winter. Penquin Books Ltd.

Engravings from *Woodcuts by Thomas Bewick and his School,* published by Dover Publications Inc., New York 1962.

My thanks to David Bromwich of the Somerset Studies Library, Taunton; the staff of Somerset Record Office; Rosemary Walker ; Dunfanaghy Workhouse Museum, Co. Donegal.

An 1830s illustration of the men's casual ward of the West London Union. This illustration forms part of a permanent exhibition at Dunfanaghy Workhouse Museum, Co. Donegal.

A 2005 photograph of part of the old Clutton workhouse, renamed 'Cambrooke' in 1905. Now private residential dwellings, its link with the past is preserved by the name Cambrook House.

WORKHOUSE

"Please, sir, do you know at what time Casterbridge Union-house closes at night?".

A neighbouring earl once said (of the workhouse) that he would give up a year's rental to have at his own door the view enjoyed by the inmates from theirs - and very probably the inmates would have given up the view for his year's rental.
Far From the Madding Crowd, Thomas Hardy.

Workhouses had their origins in the sixteenth century, operating as Houses of Correction or as institutions whose priority was the provision of relief for the poor and the disadvantaged. However, it is likely that the image most of us have of the workhouse is firmly rooted in the Victorian Age. Although the legislation that brought the Union Workhouse into being was passed in the reign of William IV, the system ran through the entire Victorian era and beyond.

There had long been a battle between the advocates of 'out-relief' (allowances) and 'in-relief' (residential). The 1834 Poor Law Amendment Act (New Poor Law) made it clear that the emphasis would be on 'in-relief'. The new Act compared unfavourably with some aspects of previous poor law legislation in force from the mid-sixteenth century until the 1830s. The New Poor Law attempted to abolish outdoor relief, which forced the sick, aged and unemployed to seek entry into the workhouse. However, in practise outdoor relief was still provided in certain circumstances, particularly in the industrialised north, where the workers were better organised than the workers in the rural south.

Conditions in the new union workhouses were made deliberately harsh and families segregated into male and female wards. Although operating a less punitive regime towards the end of the system's 95 year history the workhouse was feared and resented by the mass of people during its entire existence. The root cause of poverty, then, as now, was not always given enough consideration. This left people with a sense of injustice when affected by events outside their control.

During the five years following the passing of the 1834 Act the nation's 15,000 parishes were organised into 600 poor law unions and over 300 new workhouses built, including the Clutton Union workhouse, sited within the parish of Cameley. A plan for a union workhouse that would administer poor law provision for 29 parishes was discussed in February 1836. By the end of the year construction work on the institution had commenced at Cloud Hill and was completed in July 1838. A Board of Guardians, responsible to the Poor Law Commissioners, was charged with administering the institution under the provisions of the New Poor Law.

Residents of the new workhouses who had experience of the local poor houses would have suffered some trauma when confronted by the regimentation imposed on them by the changed system. We know that workhouses were often called 'lock-ups' by the community, as indeed were factories of the period. Harshness of working conditions both in and out of the workhouse were a feature of the Victorian and Edwardian eras and prompted agitation for legislation to prevent the worst excesses. However, it should be noted that there were many instances of workhouse staff and members of Boards of Guardians who strove to humanise the regime, sometimes bringing themselves at odds with the Poor Law Commission ands its successors the Poor Law Board (1847) and the Local Government Board (1871). The Commission was abolished following the public outcry that occured during 1845 and 1846 over the casual management of the Andover workhouse by the Board of Guardians. It came to light that conditions were so bad that the residents were driven to eat rotting bone marrow. The 'Andover Scandal', as it became known proved that the centralised nature of the Commission could not perform an adequate supervisory role.

The day to day running of a workhouse was the responsibility of the workhouse master, appointed by the Board of Guardians. One such workhouse master was James Pitt Dury who took up his duties at Clutton Union house in 1856. His great nephew, David Jones, wrote an article in the autumn 1998 edition of *The Countryman* magazine. He informs us that James Dury, a schoolmaster, operated as paternal a regime as possible within the strict limits imposed by the legislation. It appears that there was a vocational dimension to the tasks he performed. James Dury was well aware of the bleaker side of some workhouses; his grandmother, Elizabeth Dury, died a miserable death in Chertsey Workhouse in 1849. David Jones makes the valid point that this event was probably influential in the way James Dury interpreted his role.

One of the most pernicious aspects of the New Poor Law was the breaking up of families who entered the workhouse. Although obliged by law to apply this measure James Dury was scrupulous in ensuring that the children received an education, however rudimentary this may have been. Aware of the harmful effects that a workhouse environment could have on children James Dury made efforts to board out the younger ones to foster parents. The Clutton Union Board of Guardians pursued a boarded out policy for some children well into the twentieth century, as the following entry from one of the Board's minute books reveals.......

15 June 1928. Mrs Beagle reported that she had inspected the home of Kitti White (foster child), which was in every way satisfactory except that the house is old and the foster parents over 80.

It is debatable of course whether foster care placements that removed the children from the workhouse environment was less traumatic than separation from their parents.

Clutton Union-house also gave temporary shelter to those travelling in search of work or to those who had been forced into a life of vagrancy. James Dury was sensitive to the needs of these (often) friendless people and took a special interest in them. He was eventually successful in securing permission from the Board of Guardians to increase their food allowance. His efforts to encourage the more affluent members of the local community to take an interest in the work of the Union-house often paid dividends, improving the quality of life of some residents.

In general, the Boards of Guardians of urban workhouses were very rigid in the application of the New Poor Law. In contrast, again in general, the Boards of Guardians of rural workhouses could often be very enlightened. For example, in 1905 the Board of Guardians of the Clutton Union discussed the desirability of a change of name for the institution, to remove the stigma from children born there. The name of 'Cambrooke' was agreed upon which enabled the children to have 'Born at Cambrooke' entered on their birth certificates, as opposed to 'Born at Clutton Workhouse'.

James Dury remained workhouse master until his death in 1894. In James Dury we see a workhouse master who strove to be sensitive in his duties. Nevertheless, the system, being flawed from the beginning could still be harsh and unforgiving. Punishments were part and parcel of the regime and varied according to age, gender and seriousness of the offence/infringement. Sanctions could take the form of corporal punishment, denial of food or being locked up (within the workhouse). Denial of food had a long history as a sanction and was still in use in the 1900s. Operating to a strict budget the needs of residents were often unmet, including adequate medical care for the children. In 1860 James Dury reported that many of the infants were in need of nursing and special diet.

As mentioned earlier in this short study the workhouse system became less punitive by the early twentieth century. By this time the children in Clutton workhouse were attending Cameley village school and entering into the life of the community. In 1917 the visiting Inspector reported that....

the children were well cared for and happy.

However, by the 1920s it became evident that a major over-haul of welfare provision was necessary. There was a growing reluctance by Boards of Guardians and workhouse

Cameley old village school, Temple Cloud, once attended by children resident at the workhouse. Now a private residence, the school clock has been restored to working order. The new school is still situated in Temple Cloud.

masters to implement the more harsh provisions of the Poor Law; ways were sometimes found to circumvent the law if compliance led to hardship or trauma. In the winter edition of the 1995/6 *Country Origins* there is a human and interesting account of how, in 1929, two guardians and a workhouse master colluded against the Poor Law to relieve the suffering of four elderly men who fell victim to a strict adherence of the law. The events took place in the counties of Worcestershire and Gloucestershire. Administrative changes led to the four men, who were happily settled in a particular workhouse, being transferred against their will to another establishment, even though two of the men, recorded as Spider Winnet and Neil Allan, had permanent jobs within the system. One of their former guardians, Lady Norah Fitzherbert, visited the men in their new placement and found them in distressed circumstances.

A plan was hatched between Lady Norah and the workhouse master whereby he would release the men. By this means they were given the status (or non-status) of vagrants. They were picked up on the road by a Mr. Archer (another guardian) and after giving them a meal in his own home drove them to their former workhouse and booked them into the casual ward (a legal provision). They were met there by Lady Norah who reported a thankful return. A meeting of the Board of Guardians approved long term placements for the 'new' residents. Of course the local government board (had it come to their attention) could have reversed this decision, but by 1929 the Poor Law as a legal entity was nearing its end. Sections of the 1929 Local Government Act provided for the almost total reorganisation of the 1834 Poor Law Ammendment Act.

One factor in the decline of the workhouse system was the provision in 1908 of old age pensions. This enabled many elderly people to survive outside the workhouse; the pension could be viewed as 'out-relief', which meant that the government itself was undermining its own system. Therefore it was only a matter ot time before this change of direction in welfare provision culminated in the 1929 Act. Implementation of the new Act commenced in 1930 and led to the needs of the workhouse residents being properly assessed. The Board of Guardians of the Clutton Union was abolished in 1930, the last meeting taking place at 11am on Friday, the 28th March of that year. The Board was replaced by a Guardians Committee which first met on the 13th May 1930. By 1933 all the children resident in the workhouse and still in need of care were transferred to a children's home in Keynsham.

The last remnants of the poor law were discarded with the passing of the 1948 National Assistance Act. This Act was a vital component in the formation of the welfare state as we know it today (or perhaps more accurately as we knew it up until 1997). Cambrook House continued as a public assistance facility under the provisions of the 1929 Local Government Act until a change of use into a National Health Service hospital; the buildings have now been modernised into residential dwellings.*

The training ship 'Formidable', a former 'Ship of the Line', moored off Portishead, Somerset. Classified as an Industrial Training School this facility was founded in 1869 to assist boys who were suffering the rigours of destitution. Orphan boys resident in Clutton workhouse were eligible for admission into the school. T S Formidable became a shore establishment in 1903. A study of T S Formidable, by Tess Green, can be found in the Fiducia Press publication 'Past Somerset Times, Vol. 1'.

*An early 20th century photograph of the workhouse can be seen in *Hinton Blewett Village Life 1840s-1940s*, by Rosemary Walker, published by Fiducia Press.

TWO POOR LAW TALES

With the passing of time some Boards of Guardians (but by no means all) started to test the system in order to humanise the Poor Law. A good example of this occured in 1870 when Roland and Betsy Jones of Hen Hafod, Merioneth, were admitted into the Bala workhouse. A strict adherance to the provisions of the Poor Law required them to be separated and placed in male and female wards. Recognising the cruelty in this the Guardians broke with the system and found space within the workhouse for them to live in a room of their own, thereby easing the trauma of a workhouse placement after years of independence.

This growing willingness of some Boards of Guardians to demonstrate their independence did little to remove the stigma attached to admittance into the workhouse. This can be illustrated by the circumstances of James Minns (known locally as 'Rough Jimmy'), a Norfolk woodcutter. In 1901, at the age of 75 years he was still working to maintain himself. His failing eyesight meant that he could no longer perform the full range of tasks associated with his craft. At best he survived at subsistance level only. When he failed to reach even this level the authorities arranged for James to be admitted to the workhouse, a move steadfastly resisted by this independent minded craftsman. He stated that he would rather lie down and die on the side of the road. Thankfully the squire came to his aid, James accepting his offer of a free cottage and an allowance of a shilling a week for life. This change of fortune allowed James to continue working at his own pace. It is likely that James did not look on the squire's involvement as charity but as a just reward for years of hard work, a pension in all but name.

Other Titles from Fiducia Press:

Southville, People and Places
A fascinating history of a South Bristol District. **£5.00**

Past Somerset Times. Volume 1
A new series featuring 20 illustrated studies of Somerset's rich history. **£5.00**

Fussells Ironworks, Mells
A history (1744 -1895). **£5.00**

The Glastonbury Canal
Somerset's lost navigation. **£5.00**

The Coaching Era
Road travel before the railways. **£6.50**

The Parrett Navigation
River trade into the heart of Somerset. **£4.00**

Recollections of Chew Magna
A decade to remember. 1930 - 40. **£5.00**

Exploring the Smaller Towns of Somerset. £5.00

The Gentle Giants Bristol Shire Horses / Timber Haulage. **£3.00**

Miners' Memories
A South Bristol Story. **£3.00**

Great Railway Battles. £19.95

The Severn Tunnel
A vivid account by it's engineer of the construction . **£19.95**

LMS Reflections. £10.95

Paddington - GW Gateway. **£11.95**

Views of Labour and Gold
A book on political and moral economy by William Barnes. First published in 1859. **£10.00**

Recollections of Jazz in Bristol
A rich slice of musical history. **£10.00**

Dave Collett Blues
A selection of his words and music. **£5.00**

Tracts from the Tracks by Mark Griffiths.
The Ridgeway Poems. **£5.00**

Manly Monodes by Tom Lamb.
26 Alliterative poems by the Scottish poet. **£3.00**

Orra : A Lapland Tale by William Barnes. First published in 1822. **£7.00**

A Tri-cycle of Poems by Clorinda Parfitt. **£5.00**

A Walk Around Chew Magna by Mary and Ian Durham. **£6.00**

Healing Waters The Mineral Springs and Small Spas of Somerset. **£4.00**

Coming shortly......
Hinton Blewett Village Life 1840s-1940s.

All orders post free from Fiducia Press,
10 Fairfield Road,
Southville, Bristol BS3 1 LG
Tel: 0117 9852795 & 0117 9713609